A GALLERY
OF CHILDREN

PORTRAITS FROM
THE NATIONAL
GALLERY OF ART

Text by MARIAN KING

J. B. LIPPINCOTT COMPANY *Philadelphia • New York*

To Andrew W. Mellon
who made it possible for the men, women, and children of
the United States of America to have their own National
Gallery of Art.

Library of Congress Catalog Card Number 55-7987
Copyright 1955
By Marian King
Printed in the United States of America

Foreword

Marian King has a gift for vivid characterization, based on careful research not only of such facts as can be ascertained concerning the subject of her story but also about the life of the time. She has, in addition, a special talent for bringing to life the personalities of children and young people who have long since become part of history and in the process have acquired a fixed outline that accords with legend but not always with the facts of their lives. Thus she has written of the young King David, of Joseph, of Elizabeth the Tudor Princess, and of Mary, Queen of Scots. And she has written in a manner that appeals to adults no less than to her young readers for whom the books are primarily intended.

Now she has assembled reproductions of famous paintings of children in the National Gallery of Art and has written a concise description of each painting, together with an account of its history and an interpretation of the personalities involved.

We are glad to have such a book published and hope that, as a result, the enjoyment of visitors to the National Gallery may be increased and that the paintings may become better known to the people of this country to whom they belong. This, we know, is Miss King's wish in writing the book; and it is also in accord with the intentions of the donors to whose generosity we owe the National Gallery and its collections.

Washington
February 1955

DAVID E. FINLEY
Director, National Gallery of Art

Author's Note

I wish to express my sincere appreciation for the valuable cooperation rendered me by the following of the National Gallery of Art: The Director, Mr. David E. Finley; The Chief Curator, Mr. John Walker and his excellent staff; The Secretary-Treasurer and General Counsel, Mr. Huntington Cairns; The Assistant Director, Mr. Macgill James and the Library Associates. A special expression of gratitude is due Mr. William P. Campbell, Museum Curator, for his generous assistance.

Contents

Portrait of a Youth
by Giovanni Antonio Boltraffio (1467-1516)
Italian School   Ralph and Mary Booth Collection

Here is a boy in his early teens but who looks older than his years. What could have made him this way must, of course, remain unknown, but perhaps it is brought about by the empty sleeve pinned to the shoulder—for apparently the boy has lost his right arm.

There is warm color in this portrait by Boltraffio. Dark brown hair frames the boy's full face and falls below his shoulders. His clothing is rich and tastefully chosen. His white silken blouse is conspicuous against the slashed terracotta doublet. The blouse is finely pleated at the neck and bound with a delicately embroidered band. A black velvet hat casts a tiny shadow on the forehead above the widely spaced hazel eyes.

When he painted *The Portrait of a Youth,* probably shortly before the year 1500, Giovanni Antonio Boltraffio was in Milan, which was at the time one of the liveliest art centers of Italy. The great artist, Leonardo da Vinci, was a member of the court. The Duke of Milan, Lodovico Il Moro, had persuaded him to enter his service. Under Leonardo had grown up in Milan a school of painters who slavishly imitated his style of painting but with little of his genius. Among the best of this group was Boltraffio, an artist who on occasion, as in *The Portrait of a Youth,* rose to inspired heights. Whether or not he had more than the painter's acquaintance with his sitter is not known. However, he could not have painted a more sympathetic portrait of this boy, who is seen today with all the charm and appeal that he had when he looked so trustingly at the artist almost five hundred years ago.

Panel 18⁷⁄₁₆″ x 13¾″. Painted c. 1500.

Ranuccio Farnese
by Titian (1477?-1576)
Venetian School   Samuel H. Kress Collection

Shortly before Titian painted this majestic portrait of eleven-year-old Ranuccio Farnese, the boy's close relative, Pope Paul III, had sent him to Venice as Prior of San Giovanni dei Forlani, Priory of the Knights of Malta. That Ranuccio was connected with the order is shown by the silver-white Maltese cross he wears. The boy's cheeks are a warm pink reflection of the red-purple slashed doublet worn under his black velvet robe. The large dark eyes are arresting and give to the sensitive face an expression of intelligence. The lips are soft and full. The youthful roundness of the cheeks is set off by the narrow white ruff circling the neck. One hand is not visible. The other, holding gloves, is a pleasing balance for the Maltese cross.

The portrait so impressed two important churchmen that they invited Titian to the Papal Court in Rome where he painted Pope Paul III and other members of the family.

Titian was still a boy when he left his father's home in Pieve di Cadore for Venice. It was here that he was apprenticed to the famous Venetian painters, Gentile and Giovanni Bellini. The public took notice of Titian for the first time when in 1508 he assisted the artist Giorgione with the decorating of the Fondaco dei Tedeschi, a warehouse for German merchants. Following the deaths of Giorgione in 1510 and Giovanni Bellini in 1516 the way was clear for Titian in Venice.

By 1530 Titian was the undisputed leader of Italian art and from that time on his life was a succession of triumphs. When young Ranuccio Farnese sat for his portrait about 1542, Titian had already been made court painter to Charles V, whose portrait he painted in Bologna in 1533. The royal appointment brought international recognition. He also painted and was favored by Philip II of Spain who was suing for the hand of Queen Mary Tudor, daughter of Henry VIII of England and Catherine of Aragon.

Titian was well known for his portraits but his paintings of religious and mythological subjects were famous, too.

Canvas 35¼" x 29". Painted 1542.

A Prince of Saxony
by Lucas Cranach, the Elder (1472-1553)
German School   Ralph and Mary Booth Collection

Lucas Cranach, the Elder, was born in upper Franconia, Germany, in 1472 and began his art training under his father. Little is known of his early life except that he married the daughter of a burgher of Gotha, where he owned a house. Of his three sons, one, Lucas Cranach, the Younger, became his assistant.

In 1504 he settled in Wittenberg as court painter to Frederick the Wise, Elector of Saxony. Cranach painted many portraits and altarpieces, designed woodcuts, engraved copper plates and drafted dies for the mint. He had been at court four years when the elector gave him the right to a device, a winged serpent, which he used as his signature.

This portrait of a Saxon prince was painted thirteen years after Cranach came to Wittenberg. There is a fascination about this boy. His wavy blond hair is subtly varied from light to shade to express the roundness of the head. The delicate wreath is fashioned of golden wire, pearls, and precious stones. But most entrancing are those gray-blue eyes which are so firmly fixed on the observer. With uncertainty the young prince's left hand clutches the lapel of his outer robe as if he is not yet accustomed to the feel and proper set of his princely garments.

Frederick the Wise was a generous benefactor to his court painter. He gave Cranach a printer's patent and reserved for him the exclusive right to print Bibles—which brought him a good income. Frederick granted him as well a monopoly on the sale of medicines in Wittenberg.

It was at Frederick's request that Cranach paid a visit to The Netherlands. Here he gained new honors, for he was commissioned to paint the portraits of the Emperor Maximilian and the young prince who later became Charles V.

After the death of Frederick the Wise, Cranach served two of the elector's successors with equal devotion. Cranach himself died in 1553 in Weimar, a city later made famous by the German poet, Goethe.

Canvas 17⅛" x 13½". Painted c. 1517.

Edward VI as a Child
by Hans Holbein, the Younger (1497-1543)
German School Mellon Collection

It is said that when a noble complained to King Henry the VIII of England of his favoritism for Holbein, the monarch retorted, "My lord, know that of seven peasants I can easily make seven earls, but of the seven earls, I cannot make one Holbein."

This portrait of the king's son, who became Edward VI, is accepted as the one presented by Hans Holbein, the Younger, on New Year's Day, 1539, to the boy's illustrious father. So moved was the king by Holbein's gift that he presented him with a silver cup in exchange.

It was no wonder that Henry was pleased with the portrait. Even at that early age it could be seen that the physical likeness between father and son was decidedly marked. Edward wears a miniature replica of a grown-up's costume. His crimson velvet doublet has slashed sleeves; bodice and tunic are trimmed with bands of the same gold brocade as the inner sleeves. White ruffs are at the wrists and gold embroidery encircles the neckline of his shirt. The red velvet bonnet with its embroidery and ostrich plume perches gaily over the close-fitting coif. His little hand is raised in a kingly salute.

Love and hope had gone into the portrait's Latin inscription. "Little one, emulate thy father; become heir to the virtue of him whose peer the world does not possess. Heaven and earth could hardly produce a son to surpass in glory such a father. Do but match in full thy parent's deeds and men can ask no more. Shouldst thou surpass him, thou hast outstript all kings the world revered in ages past." The flattering counsel was in vain. On July 6, 1553, in his sixteenth year, Edward VI, King of England, died.

Hans Holbein, the Younger, was born in Germany, the son of a painter who was his first art teacher. At eighteen, young Holbein went to Basel, Switzerland, where he practiced his profession for the next eleven years. When he was twenty-nine, he went to England for the first time with a letter of introduction to Sir Thomas More from his early patron and friend, the Dutch scholar, Erasmus. During his two-year stay in England he painted Sir Thomas and his family and other important personages. Then again, after several years of inadequate employment in Switzerland, he returned with fresh hope to England in 1532, where four years later he became court painter to Henry VIII. At the height of his success, Holbein fell victim to the plague which was sweeping London and died at the age of forty-six.

Panel 22⅜" x 17⅜". Painted 1538.

PARVVLE PATRISSA, PATRIÆ VIRTVTIS ET HÆRES
ESTO, NIHIL MAIVS MAXIMVS ORBIS HABET.
GNATVM VIX POSSVNT COELVM ET NATVRA DEDISSE,
HVIVS QVEM PATRIS, VICTVS HONORET HONOS,
ÆQVATO TANTVM, TANTI TV FACTA PARENTIS,
VOTA HOMINVM, VIX QVO PROGREDIANTVR, HABENT
VINCITO, VICISTI. QVOT REGES PRISCVS ADORAT
ORBIS, NEC TE QVI VINCERE POSSIT, ERIT.

Clelia Cattaneo, Daughter of Marchesa Elena Grimaldi

by Sir Anthony Van Dyck (1599-1641)

Flemish School   Widener Collection

In this portrait by Anthony Van Dyck, Clelia Cattaneo, daughter of Marchesa Elena Grimaldi and Marchese Nicola Cattaneo, stands at the top of a step in front of a stool upholstered in red velvet and tasseled gold braid, against the shadowy outlines of a column. The child's hands cast a shadow on the sheer material of the pinafore, allowing the dark color of the undergarment to show through. There is a trace of self-consciousness about the little girl's face; one gets a feeling that the painter caught here the vividness for which he strove. The clutching of the fruit in Clelia's chubby hands is a gesture wholly natural and childlike. Her padded garment stands out stiffly. She is obviously well protected from Genoa's chill winds. The spun gold of her hair is caught in light.

Anthony Van Dyck, who was born in Antwerp, was only a boy of ten when he was apprenticed to the painter Hendrik van Balen. At the age of sixteen Van Dyck had become an independent painter, working at portraits and at heads of Christ and the Apostles. Three years later the Guild of St. Luke admitted him as a full member, an unusual honor for so young an artist. By that time Rubens had welcomed this talented young man as an assistant.

During the following year Van Dyck spent some time at the court of James I of England. Following a brief visit to Flanders, the artist's cherished desire to study the great masters was realized in a visit to Italy.

After his return to his homeland, Van Dyck rivaled his former master, Rubens. But when in 1632 an invitation came from Charles I, now on the throne of England, to be his court painter, Van Dyck again crossed the Channel. At the king's expense he was lodged in apartments in Blackfriars, given a country house in Kent, and knighted as "Sir Anthony Vandike, principalle Paynter in ordinary to their Majesties." During the eight years spent at the court of Charles I, Sir Anthony painted the royal family and many of the nobility.

After a brief visit to the Continent, Van Dyck returned to England, where he died shortly afterward, at the age of forty-two. His tomb in old St. Paul's Cathedral was destroyed with the building in the Great Fire of 1666.

Canvas 48⅛" x 33⅛". Painted 1623

A Girl with a Broom
by Rembrandt van Ryn (1606-1669)
Dutch School   Mellon Collection

When Rembrandt's father became convinced that his son wanted to be a painter, the fifteen-year-old boy went to Amsterdam to study under Pieter Lastman. Although his apprenticeship continued only six months, it was Lastman's example that gave the boy the desire to paint Biblical subjects. Upon Rembrandt's return to Leyden, he set himself up as an independent painter. Having achieved considerable recognition, he went again to Amsterdam to seek the greater opportunities that presented themselves in the larger city. Here he lived for the remainder of his life.

Rembrandt places his people before one in a close intimate way; they exist as individuals with personal dignity. In the forthright gaze of the little Dutch girl one senses a comfortable self-assurance. In just such a manner, this child might have rested, leaning on a wooden fence, her sturdy arms folded across her broom. An area of light brings out her face which reflects the red of her bodice. The dark eyes are alert. The well-developed hands show plainly that she is used to hard work.

The young girl with her broom and overturned brass pail could have been a neighbor's child, or one who worked in the artist's household, or perhaps the daughter of one of Rembrandt's friends.

About 1640 Rembrandt's popularity as a painter began to wane. Artistic taste was beginning to favor the elegant style of Van Dyck. Ten years before his death Rembrandt was forced to sell all he had. Until his death he lived in poverty, and yet most of his finest painting belongs to these difficult years.

       Canvas 42¼" x 36⅛". Painted 1651.

The Bedroom
by Pieter de Hooch (1629-c. 1683)
Dutch School   Widener Collection

Certain Dutch painters of the seventeenth century are called "Little Masters." They were superlative craftsmen and are called "little" only because they limited themselves in the types of subject matter they pictured. They specialized in landscapes, or seascapes, or they were painters of portraits, still lifes, or interior scenes. As a group their pictures reflect the life of a people as the art of no other period or area has done.

Among the best of the "Little Masters" is Pieter de Hooch. His interior scenes are considered among the finest ever painted. In *The Bedroom* this artist has, as usual, shown a very simple event—a child interrupts her mother who is making the bed in the curtained alcove behind her. The picture tells much about the Dutch home, costume, and manner of life of that day; but de Hooch's interest was less in the scene itself than in the creation of a feeling of light and air within the space he painted. This is one of the most difficult things for a painter to do, and here de Hooch excelled.

Little is known of de Hooch's life. He was born in Rotterdam in 1629, the son of a mason. By 1655, when he probably settled in Delft, he was already an accomplished artist. In the next twelve years, during which *The Bedroom* was painted, he did his best work. De Hooch was married in Delft, and had two children. His wife and daughter are undoubtedly the two figures in *The Bedroom*. They appear often in his paintings, as does the bedroom itself, which surely was in the artist's home. After the death of his wife in 1667, de Hooch moved to Amsterdam where he died about 1683.

Canvas 20¹³⁄₁₆" x 24¹⁄₁₆". Painted c. 1660.

Soap Bubbles
By Jean-Baptiste-Siméon Chardin (1699-1779)
French School   Gift of Mrs. John W. Simpson

Jean-Baptiste-Siméon Chardin was the son of a French cabinetmaker. He first worked as an apprentice in his father's shop, but before long his talent asserted itself, and he decided to become a painter. He studied with several well-known artists. But it was not until his introduction to the works of the Dutch masters by his half-Dutch friend, Aved, that Chardin found all he longed for and needed to know about painting. In recognition of his achievement Chardin, at twenty-nine, was made a member of the Academy and was later honored by the royal patronage of Louis XV. Although Chardin's still lifes attracted attention, it was his genre (everyday life) pictures of the middle-class household of Paris, where he was born, that established his reputation.

A young boy leaning out of a window and blowing bubbles may well have seemed unimportant to painters of Chardin's day. They were mainly interested in painting the activities of ladies and gentlemen. Yet in this work of Chardin one senses the exacting care the artist has given to his scene, probably one he had witnessed many times. In this painting he has devoted himself to a careful and sympathetic study of textures and tones and harmoniously related colors. He has concentrated on a small area so intently that one feels the exclusion of the outside world. One could watch forever with the little boy, who strains to see over the window sill, the luminous bubble that will never burst.

During the last twenty-five years of his life Chardin devoted himself almost entirely to painting still life. Although in his own day these still lifes did not receive the acclaim of his genre painting, today they are considered at least equally important.

Canvas 36⅝" x 29⅝". Painted c. 1740.

The Magic Lantern
by Charles-Amédée-Philippe Van Loo (1719-1795)
French School   Gift of Mrs. Robert W. Schuette

There is a feeling of peace in this scene of three alert interested children grouped together by Charles-Amédée-Philippe Van Loo. They are three of the artist's nine children and he has framed them, as if in a window, by a wreath carved in stone. The older girl's face is delicate, a somewhat paler reflection of her little sister's healthy glow. Her carefully curled and powdered hair falls gently over a fragile, blue-gray scarf. In her graceful, yet strong, hands she supports her sister. Behind them appears a delicate-featured boy who reaches out through the frame to hold a wooden box with an eyepiece. In the gloom of the shadow, the color of his jacket barely shows as gold.

Apparently there was no controversy over a career in art for Van Loo, for the family had been artists for generations and the profession was taken for granted. His father, a successful painter in France, was his first teacher. At nineteen the precocious boy won the *grand prix* at the Royal Academy in Paris. There followed three and a half years of study in Rome, then two years painting with his father in Aix, near Marseilles. In 1747, at the age of twenty-eight, Van Loo married his cousin, and during the same year was named a member of the Royal Academy. A year later he was honored by being made court painter to Frederick the Great in Berlin. While living in this city, in 1764, he painted *The Magic Lantern.*

Although Van Loo's reputation today rests on his portraits, royal orders in Berlin kept him busy with many other projects. There were huge decorative paintings and tapestry designs for various palaces. Van Loo worked in Berlin until 1769, when he returned to Paris to stay. The next year he was appointed professor at the Royal Academy, and in 1790 he became its assistant rector. He died at the age of seventy-six.

Canvas 34⅞" x 34⅞". Painted 1764.

Group Portrait

by François-Hubert Drouais (1727-1775)
French School   Samuel H. Kress Collection

At the court of Louis XV, François-Hubert Drouais was in great demand not only as a painter of adults but also of children. In tune with the times, he broke away from the formally posed portrait. He seems to have caught his sitters unaware in the midst of some activity. His paintings hide nothing; they are enriched with a variety of objects as if he enjoyed making full use of his canvas. Inevitably the people in his paintings look their best; they are elegant, gracious, and usually handsome.

In the *Group Portrait,* one of Drouais' most important works, the artist signs and dates the painting, April 1, 1756, on the lid of the box on the floor. In Drouais' day, the first of April was a day on which gifts and good wishes were exchanged. The artist gives here a glimpse of just such a happy family scene.

One can see the rich silks and know that they would rustle with each movement of the wearer. The blue-green drapery has been pulled aside to let in the morning light. The small girl in a blue dress, her arms filled with flowers, waits patiently while her mother fastens an ornament to her heavily powdered hair. An open powder box on the dressing table suggests that her mother has just finished doing her own hair. The soft white dressing jacket was to protect her lavender bodice and golden skirt from falling powder. The gentleman in his brown brocaded coat watches his wife and daughter approvingly. In his hand he still holds his April-the-first greeting.

Most of François-Hubert Drouais' life was spent in Paris, where he was born. His father, Hubert Drouais, was his first art teacher. Later he studied successively under Carle van Loo, Natoire, and Boucher. In his late twenties he was admitted to the Academy and first exhibited at the *Salon.* It was this recognition that brought him to the attention of the court of Louis XV, where he soon was fully occupied painting members of the royal family and the nobility.

Canvas 96" x 76⅝". Painted 1756.

Lady Caroline Howard
by Sir Joshua Reynolds (1723-1792)
British School   Mellon Collection

Joshua Reynolds was not yet a well-known painter when, at twenty-nine, he returned to England from Italy with a determination to match the effects of the old masters. Immediately his brilliant new style and his delightful personality made him the most popular painter of the day.

Not only was Reynolds successful in the portrayal of adults, but he was able to paint children with understanding. This genius is shown in the portrait of seven-year-old Lady Caroline Howard, who later became Lady Cawdor. She is represented formally, against an artificial landscape, seemingly absorbed in the pink rose she fingers. The painting of her elegant costume is a deft performance in black and white, relieved only by pink in the headdress and the blue sash. In spite of its formality and elegance, it is, before everything else, a portrait of the freshness of youth.

In addition to being the leading figure in the art world of England, Reynolds knew many of the famous men of his day. His abilities were given official recognition when in 1768, at the age of forty-five, he was elected first president of the Royal Academy, the body before which he was to deliver his famous *Discourses*. And a few months later he was knighted by George III, who in 1784 honored him further by appointing him painter to the Crown. Sir Joshua continued to produce large numbers of portraits until 1790 when he had to stop because of ailing health and failing eyesight. Two years later he died.

Canvas 56¼" x 44½". Painted c. 1778.

Lady Caroline Howard
Lady Cawdor

Miss Willoughby
by George Romney (1734-1802)
British School   Mellon Collection

In 1775, George Romney returned to London after a two-year's study of the Italian masters. He settled in a fashionable section of London, and soon had a practice that made him the rival of Sir Joshua Reynolds. Between 1781 and 1783, in eight sittings, Romney painted *Miss Willoughby*.

Against a background of autumn sky and foliage the artist has posed little Miss Willoughby. She stands completely relaxed, toying with the pink ribbons of her broad-brimmed hat. In keeping with her simplicity are her plain white dress and pink sash. Dark hair frames her wholesome features. Young and pretty Miss Willoughboy is a type rather than a specific personality.

George Romney was born at Dalton-in-Furness, England. At the age of ten he began working for his father, a cabinetmaker. Young Romney occupied his leisure time carving wood figures, playing a violin he had made himself and sketching the workmen in his father's shop. Impressed by the boy's talent for drawing, the elder Romney apprenticed his son at the age of nineteen to a little-known painter at Kendal, in Westmorland County.

In 1756 Romney married the daughter of his landlady, who had nursed him through a serious illness. After practicing six years as an itinerant painter in the northern counties of England, Romney left his wife and son—whom he saw only occasionally during the next thirty-seven years—to seek his fortune in London. Here his abilities were soon recognized.

Romney remained a successful painter in London until 1799, when failing health caused him to retire to his home in Kendal, "where he had the comfort," as his biographer and friend, William Hayley, tells us, "of finding an attentive affectionate nurse, in a most exemplary wife, who had never been irritated to an act of unkindness, or an expression of reproach, by his years of absence and neglect."

Canvas 36⅛" x 28". Painted 1781-1783.

The Binning Children

by Sir Henry Raeburn (1756-1823)

British School   Gift of Miss Jean Simpson

Sir Henry Raeburn is generally considered the foremost portrait painter of Scotland. He was born in Stockbridge, then a suburb of Edinburgh. At six he was orphaned. At fifteen he was apprenticed to a goldsmith. This was the most fortunate turn of his life, for not only did Raeburn learn the craftsmanship of that trade, but two of the goldsmith's friends started him on his career. From a seal engraver he had his first art lesson; from David Martin, the leading portraitist of Edinburgh, he received advice in portrait painting.

By twenty-two, Raeburn had achieved considerable reputation in his native town and was devoting full time to portraiture. One notable commission was to paint the young widow of Count Leslie whom he had seen and admired from afar, but had not met. Within a month the handsome painter and his lovely sitter were married. In 1785, armed with letters from Sir Joshua Reynolds, President of the Royal Academy in London, Raeburn and his wife set out for Rome where the artist hoped to refine his style. He returned to Edinburgh in 1787 where he remained the rest of his life, the acknowledged first painter of Scotland. He was President of the Society of Artists in Edinburgh and member of the Royal Academy in London. Finally, in 1822, Raeburn was knighted by George IV.

The portrait of *The Binning Children,* painted about 1811, is one of Raeburn's most winning. One finds two boys posed in an artificial autumn landscape. Their faces are scrubbed, their pink cheeks blooming. They are immaculate in matching plum-brown suits, freshly pleated collars, clean white stockings properly held up, and well shined shoes. That this tidiness was not the usual state of the boys is suggested by their tousled soft brown hair.

This portrait shows how easily Raeburn painted. There is nothing superfluous, nothing gone over. Broad confident brush strokes indicate that to the artist painting had beome as natural as breathing, that what he saw with his mind flowed from his brush onto the canvas effortlessly and with precision.

Canvas 50⅝" x 40⅜". Painted c. 1811.

The Washington Family
by Edward Savage (1761-1817)
American School   Mellon Collection

In this painting of *The Washington Family* one can see just how these historical persons really looked. In working out the composition Edward Savage relied on the traditional device of columns and drapery, handed down from the days of Van Dyck. This gives a stage-like background against which the family appears dignified and important. With the elements of this convention the artist combines the local scene of the Potomac, as viewed from Mt. Vernon.

Washington's sword and cocked hat remind one of his military career. Mrs. Washington, in the light gray cap, black lace shawl and gray silk dress, points with her fan to the "grand avenue" on L'Enfant's plan of the nation's new capital. Lost in thought General Washington rests his arm on the shoulder of George Washington Parke Custis, grandson of his wife by a former marriage. The boy's sister, Eleanor Parke Custis, stands beside their grandmother, Martha Custis Washington. Behind them, is a trusted servant, Billy Lee.

The painter, Edward Savage, was born in Princeton, Massachusetts. It is generally believed that he received his early training as a goldsmith, and in his twenties turned to painting. In 1789, President Willard of Harvard College sent Savage to George Washington with a letter requesting that the general sit for a portrait.

It was during 1789, while Savage was working on the portrait, that he began his sketches for *The Washington Family*. The painting, however, was not finished until seven years later. Meanwhile Savage had worked in London for three years. Here he engraved plates in mezzotint and in stipple.

Edward Savage continued to paint and make engravings of prominent personages until his death in 1817.

Canvas 84⅜" x 111⅞". Painted 1789-1796.

Victor Guye

by Francisco José de Goya y Lucientes (1746-1828)

Spanish School   Lent by Charles B. Harding, Catharine H. Tailer, and Laura Harding

Victor Guye was the tousle-haired court page of Joseph Bonaparte, who had become ruler of French-conquered Spain in 1808. If one analyzes his features, he is a homely boy. The eyes are too far apart, the nose too large and blunt, the mouth too small. Yet what an appeal there is in the face that stares out so unhappily from the canvas! The wide eyes plead for understanding, and the mouth shows his anxiety. Young Victor is clad all in black and weighed down under a mass of gold braid. Automatically, as if in obedience to a command, he holds an open book. To emphasize his loneliness he is made to stand in an indefinite space against a deep red-brown darkness—alone but for his shadow. It is characteristic of Goya that he should be so outspoken about the features of this small boy, and just as characteristic that he tell so much about his inner feelings. But there is a sense of compassion here that is absent from most of Goya's portraits.

Fact and fiction in the life of Francisco José de Goya y Lucientes are frequently hard to separate. He was born in 1746 in a very small town near Saragossa in Spain. Early he gave evidence of an artistic ability and at the age of fourteen was apprenticed to an undistinguished painter in Saragossa. Apparently he was a reckless youth, for a series of escapades caused him to move often. He studied in Madrid under Francisco Bayeu, a painter at the court. Then followed a year in Rome. By 1775 Goya seems to have settled down. He was back in Madrid and married to Josefa Bayeu, the sister of his former teacher. Shortly he received a royal commission to design a tapestry, the first of a famous series he was to execute. From that time on he received many honors and in 1799 was made First Court Painter to Charles IV.

Between 1808 and 1812, Goya served the court of the French conquerors of Spain, painting at this time the portrait of Victor Guye, a nephew of a general of the French army. It was also during this period that Goya made a long series of etchings that showed his hatred of war. These were an appalling commentary on the atrocities and starvation resulting from the French invasion.

In 1824 he went to Bordeaux, France, for his health. Here he continued to paint and etch, and to experiment with the new technique of lithography. At this time a friend said that he was "deaf, aged, awkward and weak . . . but is quite contented and wants to see people." Goya was still active and concerned with human affairs when he died in Bordeaux at the age of eighty-two.

Canvas 42" x 33½". Painted 1810.

Algerian Child
by Eugène Delacroix (1798-1863)
French School   Chester Dale Collection

Eugène Delacroix's portrait of the *Algerian Child* was probably painted when the artist visited Morocco in 1832. The child is shown wearing a dull gold-colored scarf over a dark outergarment ornamented at the neck with a gold pin. Her headdress is fashioned of red material, trimmed with bright red tassels. Her face is framed by black hair and over the forehead hang unevenly-parted bangs. Her olive complexion has a healthy glow. Dark, wide set eyes are thoughtful. The mouth is straight, thin lipped and smiling. Gold looped earrings adorn her ears.

Eugène Delacroix was born of a prominent family at Charenton-Saint-Maurice, near Paris, in 1798. Apparently he did not decide definitely upon a career in art until an unsuccessful lawsuit involving family property left him penniless in 1819. Once decided, however, he was soon recognized as a figure to contend with. As early as 1822, at the age of twenty-four, he exhibited his *Dante and Virgil* which impressed everyone who saw it at the *Salon*. The painting was purchased by the government.

Delacroix was always eager, always learning. In 1824 he first saw paintings by the English artist Constable, whose luminous color fascinated him. Shortly before the *Salon* of that year opened, Delacroix decided his *Massacre at Scio,* which had already been accepted by the jury, would be improved if he used Contable's technique to heighten its color. The paint was still wet on this huge canvas when the *Salon* opened. The following year Delacroix went to England where he was impressed by the paintings of Reynolds, Gainsborough, and Lawrence.

Delacroix's visit to Morocco in 1832 stirred his imagination to his last days. He filled his notebooks with sketches, some in color, some in black and white, of wedding festivities, sultans, pashas, soldiers, slaves, and horses with elaborate trappings. These sketches guided him in painting many of his later works.

Delacroix won high honors and official commissions during his lifetime. At the 1855 World's Fair in Paris, eight years before his death, he was one of two Frenchmen chosen to represent the art of his country.

Canvas 18¼" x 15". Painted c. 1832.

The Old Musician
by Edouard Manet (1832-1883)
French School   Chester Dale Collection

Edouard Manet's father intended his son for the law, but the boy was determined to be an artist. To settle the matter they compromised on a naval career, but Manet twice failed the examinations. Then Manet's father reluctantly permitted him to enter the studio of the able painter, Thomas Couture. Here he studied from time to time and without enthusiasm for six years. A more important teacher was the seventeenth-century Spanish painter, Velasquez, whose works in the Louvre, the great museum in Paris, Manet had begun to study toward the end of the 1850's. *The Old Musician* of 1862 shows this influence.

The Old Musician was not intended to picture a real event. An awkward group has assembled by chance. In the center is a musician, a picturesque character from the Polish quarter of Paris. Unkempt though he is, Manet has given him a dignity that reminds one of the philosophers and court buffoons painted by Velasquez. His cloak, as if it were a Roman toga, is thrown over his shoulder. Unseeing he gazes at the spectator, his fingers absently pluck a melody on the strings of his violin. Behind him is a top-hatted figure wrapped in a blanket, his face curiously out of focus. The model was a ragpicker who frequented the galleries of the Louvre. From behind the frame emerges a turbaned oriental in a long robe; he is rapt in thought. To the left Manet has shown two boys from the street, and a ragged barefoot girl holding her baby brother. All is brown except the blue skirt of the young girl, the green grape leaves and a few touches of blue and green. And over all is an air of unreality that sets *The Old Musician* apart from all but a few of Manet's works.

Almost from the first Manet's pictures shocked the public—they were considered coarse, ugly, vulgar. A few people, however, were immediately attracted to his vigorous manner of painting, and the novelist Zola wrote of him more than once in high praise. By the 1870's Manet had become recognized by a small group of progressive painters and collectors with insight, but the public continued to scoff. Finally in 1882 he was honored with the Cross of the Legion of Honor. The following year he died, little understood and still generally unappreciated.

Canvas 73¾" x 98". Painted 1862.

A Girl with a Watering Can
by Auguste Renoir (1841-1919)
French School   Chester Dale Collection

"A picture ought to be a lovable thing, joyous and pretty, yes, pretty. There are enough boring things in life without our fabricating still more." That was how Renoir felt about art. Whatever he painted—women, children, animals, or flowers—his pictures always expressed this belief.

A Girl with a Watering Can, one of Renoir's most popular paintings, has a lovely luminous quality. The little girl's cheeks glow pink. There is blue in her dress, in her eyes, in the white lace of her dress, and even the buttons of her shoes have a bluish cast. The red of the saucy bow on her light hair is repeated in the flowers and in the red of her lips. There is green in the grass and foliage and in the flowers. The garden path is warm with sunlight.

Auguste Renoir was born at Limoges, France, the son of a tailor. In his early years he worked in a china factory, painting delicate figures and floral patterns on porcelain. Later he found employment in decorating fans with copies of the paintings of Watteau, Boucher, and Fragonard. When he had saved enough money, Renoir entered Gleyre's studio in Paris where he began seriously to study painting. It was here that he met two great painters, Monet and Sisley, with whom a lasting friendship began.

By the time he reached his late sixties, his hands had become so crippled that he could no longer hold a brush. But Renoir was not to be denied the work that was life itself to him. With brushes strapped to his hands he continued to paint. Despite this handicap his pictures still achieved that beauty and joy which Renoir felt was essential to art.

Canvas 39½" x 28¾". Painted 1876.

The Boating Party
by Mary Cassatt (1845-1926)
American School   Chester Dale Collection

During the winter of 1893-94 on the French Riviera Mary Cassatt painted *The Boating Party*. Twenty years later she wrote Durand-Ruel, a dealer who wished to buy the picture, "I do not wish to sell it, I have already promised it to my family. . . . I have so few things to leave my nieces and nephews!"

The favorite theme of Mary Cassatt's paintings was the mother and child. In *The Boating Party* her usual study of tender love in secure surroundings is replaced by a different situation. Apparently unaccustomed to small boat travel the tense mother sits uneasily, protectively clutching her restless child, who, indifferent to the mother's concern, is determined to get off her lap.

The artist has used a skillful blending of blue, blue-green, and black, and, surprisingly, even a little pink to give movement to the water. Some of the blues in the boatman's sash echo the blues in the sea. The various greens in the woman's hat are found again in the sail, in the boat, and in the darker green of the shoreline. The pink that shows here and there in the water picks up the pink of the baby's dress and the plaid of the woman's costume.

When she was twenty-three Mary Cassatt, despite her family's disapproval, sailed for Europe to study art. After copying the old masters in Italy, Spain, Belgium, and Holland, she settled in Paris in 1874. Her paintings were shown at the *Salon* in Paris. They were chosen by a jury who were conservative in their taste. But in 1877 her entry was refused. At this point the artist, Edgar Degas, who had never met her but was impressed with her talent, asked her to exhibit with the Impressionist group. "I accepted with joy," she told her biographer. "Now I could work with absolute independence without considering the opinion of a jury. I had already recognized who were my true masters. I admired Manet, Courbet, and Degas. I took leave of conventional art—I began to live." But living was difficult. For in those days the Impressionists were scoffed at and had yet to win their battle for public acceptance. It was not until an exhibition of her work in Paris in 1893, shortly before *The Boating Party* was painted, that her reputation became secure.

In her later years Mary Cassatt spent much time and energy advising wealthy American collectors, and it is due to her keen judgment that many fine paintings by Impressionists and by old masters have come to this country. She died in France on June 19, 1926.

Canvas 35½" x 46¼". Painted 1893-1894.

Breezing Up
by Winslow Homer (1836-1910)
American School   Gift of the W. L. and May T. Mellon Foundation

During the Civil War, Winslow Homer as a war correspondent contributed sketches to *Harper's Weekly.* Out of these experiences came one of his first paintings, *Home, Sweet Home,* which was exhibited at the National Academy in New York in 1863. Three years later *Prisoners from the Front,* shown at the same Academy, was a sensational success and made its author famous overnight.

Breezing Up took three years to paint. Sun-bronzed boys like these, in their wrinkled clothes, were a common sight around Gloucester, Massachusetts. Typical, too, is the short-bearded fisherman in his vermilion shirt, half crouching as he holds the mainsheet. In the rising wind the boys have arranged themselves in order to counterbalance the tilt of the boat as it speeds along in a choppy sea. The lad stretched full length by the mast is oblivious of the spray of the bow waves, while the boy beside him, cutting a silhouette against the sky, holds on to the coaming. The light, which strikes his left hand, is caught in the gleaming scales of the fish in the bottom of the boat.

Winslow Homer's love for the sea came naturally. He was a descendant of Captain John Homer who, in the middle of the seventeenth century, sailed his craft from old England to the thriving New England seaport where Winslow Homer was born. The boy's mother was a talented water-colorist. What satisfaction she must have gained from working with her son and seeing the vigor and scope of his talent develop! His father, also recognizing his son's ability, encouraged it.

At the age of nineteen Homer was apprenticed to a lithographer. At twenty-one he established a studio of his own in Boston, where he made drawings for wood-engravings. Two years later Homer settled in New York. There he lost no time attending night classes at the National Academy of Design, where he was a frequent exhibitor.

Winslow Homer worked with equal zest in pen-and-ink, water colors, and oil. Whether he dealt with a cotton picker, with children at play, blue-uniformed soldiers, men in the fields, or with women walking along the shore, his style is both forceful and spontaneous. In Winslow Homer the American scene has a truly American painter.

Canvas 24½" x 38⅛". Painted 1873-1876.

Catherine
by Robert Henri (1865-1929)
American School   Given in memory of Mr. and Mrs. William J. Johnson

Robert Henri was summering in 1913 on Achill Island, County Mayo, Ireland, when he painted the portrait of *Catherine,* the daughter of a local fisherman. The child is pictured in a gray nondescript dress against a gray-brown background. An iris blue kerchief is knotted under her chin with the ends tucked into the neck of her frock. Her black hair, accenting the whiteness of her skin and rosy cheeks, straggles across her forehead and down each side of an oval face, in uneven pointed wisps. Young Catherine's wide eyes are thoughtful and attentive. The portrait shows her childish freshness and simplicity.

Robert Henri was born in Cincinnati, Ohio, in 1865. His family was of French, English, and Irish origin. As a young boy he traveled through western United States and was impressed by the primitive life he saw there. At twenty-one he entered the Pennsylvania Academy of Fine Arts, and two years later he left to study in Paris. Here he learned much about technique, but he did not like the rigid training. In desperation he turned to the old masters at the Louvre, and the more modern painters—Courbet, Manet, and Whistler—whom he studied on his own.

From France, Henri went to Italy and in 1891 returned to Philadelphia where he began a long and successful career of painting and teaching. After two more visits to France he settled in New York, where he was a very successful teacher at the Art Students League. He looked for the spark of greatness in all his students and encouraged them to develop their own styles. His love of people made him a natural leader in his profession. At every turn, he sought to enlarge the opportunities for American artists. Many of our best painters were among his pupils.

In the summer Henri traveled frequently in America or abroad. The people he met became the subjects of his art. He once wrote, "I seek only, wherever I go, for symbols of greatness . . . they may be found in the eyes of a child, in the movement of a gladiator, in the heart of a gypsy, in twilight in Ireland, or in the moonrise over the deserts. To hold the spirit of greatness is in my mind what the world was created for. The human body is beautiful as this spirit shines through, and art is great as it translates and embodies this spirit."

Canvas 24" x 20⅛". Painted 1913.

Bibliography

The volumes, articles, and treatises listed are only a few of the many used in connection with the writing of this book.

BAKER, C. H. COLLINS, AND MONTAGUE R. JAMES. *British Painting*. Boston: Hale, Cushman & Flint, 1933.

BERENSON, BERNARD. *The Italian Painters of the Renaissance*. London: Phaidon Press Ltd., 1952.

BURCKHARDT, JAKOB C. *The Civilization of the Renaissance in Italy*. Vienna: The Phaidon Press.

GOMBRICH, E. H. *The Story of Art*. London: Phaidon Press, Ltd., 1950

TILLEY, ARTHUR A. *Studies in the French Renaissance*. Cambridge (Eng.): The University Press, 1922.

THIEME, ULRICH AND FELIX BECKER. *Allgemeines Lexikon der bildenden Künstler*. Leipzig: E. A. Seemann, 1907-1952.

WILENSKI, R. H. *Dutch Painting*. London: Faber and Faber Ltd., 1945.
    English Painting. London: Faber and Faber Ltd., 1933.
    French Painting. Boston: Charles T. Branford Co., 1949.

RICHTER, J. P. *The Mond Collection, An Appreciation*. London: John Murray, 1910, Vol. II, 374-380.

SEGARD, ACHILLE. *Mary Cassatt*. Paris: Librairie Paul Ollendorff, 1913.

RIDDER, ANDRE DE. *J. B. S. Chardin*. Paris: Librairie Floury, 1932.

FRIEDLANDER, MAX J., and JAKOB ROSENBERG. *Die Gemälde von Lucas Cranach*. Berlin: Deutscher Verein für Kunstwissenschaft, 1932.

The Journal of Eugène Delacroix. Translated by WALTER PACH. New York: Covici-Friede, Inc., 1937.

GABILLOT, C. "Les Trois Drouais," *Gazette des Beaux-Arts*, 3e Pér., XXXIV (1905), 177-194, 288-298, 384-400; XXXV (1906), 155-174, 246-258. Paris: G. Wildenstein.

CUST, LIONEL. *Anthony Van Dyck, An Historical Study of His Life and Works*. London: George Bell & Sons, 1900.

BERUETE Y MORET, AURELIANO DE. *Goya As Portrait Painter*. Translated by SELWYN BRINTON. London, Bombay, Sydney: Constable and Company Ltd., 1922.

RYERSON, MARGERY, compiled by. *The Art Spirit by Robert Henri*. Philadelphia and New York: J. B. Lippincott, 1951.

CHAMBERLAIN, ARTHUR B. *Hans Holbein, the Younger*. 2 vols. New York: Dodd, Mead and Company, 1913.

BAKER, C. H. COLLINS. *Pieter de Hooch, Masters of Painting*. London: "The Studio," 1925.

GOODRICH, LLOYD. *Winslow Homer*. New York: published for the Whitney Museum of American Art by the Macmillan Company, 1944.

OULMONT, CHARLES. "Amédée Van Loo, Peintre Du Roi de Prusse," *Gazette des Beaux-Arts*, 4e Pér., VIII (1912), 139-150, 223-24. Paris: G. Wildenstein.

HAMILTON, GEORGE HEARD. *Manet and His Critics*. New Haven: Yale University Press, 1954.

ARMSTRONG, SIR WALTER. *Sir Henry Raeburn*. London: William Heinemann, 1901.

ROSENBERG, JAKOB. *Rembrandt*. Cambridge: Harvard University Press, 1948.

VOLLARD, AMBROISE. *Renoir, An Intimate Record*. New York: Alfred A. Knopf, 1934.

WATERHOUSE, ELLIS K. *Reynolds*. London: Kegan Paul, Trench, Trubner & Co. Ltd., 1941.

WARD, HUMPHRY, and W. ROBERTS. *Romney*. 2 vols. London, Manchester, Liverpool: Thomas Agnew & Sons. New York: Charles Scribner's Sons, 1904.

DRESSER, LOUISA. "Edward Savage, 1761-1817," *Art in America*, Vol. 40, No. 4 (1952), 157-212.

TIETZE, HANS. *Titian*. London: Phaidon Press Ltd., 1950.